Elizabeth Merttins

Loving Spirit
of Valence House

Elizabeth Merttins

Loving Spirit of Valence House

Written by Rosalind Alexander
and Deirdre Marculescu
Edited by Derek Alexander

Valence House Publications

Published in 2025 by Valence House Publications
Valence House, Becontree Avenue
Dagenham, Essex RM8 3HT

www.valencehousecollections.co.uk

ISBN 978-1-911391-14-2

Introduction and all editorial material copyright ©Valence House Publications 2025

All rights reserved. No part of this book may be reproduced or transmitted in any form or by any means, electronic or mechanical, including photocopying, recording or by any information storage or retrieval system, without permission from the Publisher in writing

Other Publications
A Brief History of Valence House (978-1-911391-12-8)
Dagenham Days (978-1-911391-08-1)

Cover Images :
reconstruction of Valence House 1690
Other images from Wikipedia and Wikicommons

Elizabeth Merttins - loving spirit of Valence House

My name is Elizabeth Merttins…perhaps you know me, or maybe you have seen me as I am often around Valence House? You see, I have lived all my life at the house and having a long story to tell I would like you to hear it – have you the time?

I was born in Valence House during 1720 but long before then the house had been owned by my grandfather Henry Merttins. When he died, Valence House was left to his son who was my father John Henry Merttins, so my earliest memories are of how he made it such a beautiful happy family home for us. That's why I want to share its wonderful story with everyone I meet.

My grandfather and father were jewellers by trade, which is always a good occupation, so we were never short of money. We had servants who were kept very busy for then there were many people living in Valence House besides our family. Thomas Collier with his family rented the attic rooms in the west wing and some of the rooms on the ground floor, but perhaps the luckier ones were my sister Mary, brother John and I, as we had a nursery and bedrooms where the walls were hung with the most beautiful tapestries.

Valence House a reconstruction as in 1690.

All round the outside of the house there was a moat which contained fish, and close by were young holm oaks and many hazel and walnut trees. In our kitchen garden we grew fresh food - vegetables, herbs and fruits, and nearby were chickens in a hen house which I loved to feed. We also had a farm with cows grazing and producing fresh milk, and of course, we had horses in the stables.

We were so lucky to be living in Dagenham with so much fresh air and far from the smoke of London. We had lots of fields, woodlands and ponds to explore, and of course, there was also the open marshland that led out to the River Thames. On sunny days, as we took long walks in the fields and through the woods, we could hear skylarks singing their beautiful song and from the edge of the marsh, we watched the lapwings perform their amazing flying displays.

Our woodland trees were mainly oak and elm which the labourers harvested for wood that was then sold as timber. The farmers worked hard too, growing and harvesting the crops from the fields and ours was such a wonderful community, working and playing together on the farms and land.

My father often had friends come down from London who stayed overnight. They shared and enjoyed many activities including hunting, fishing, hawking and fowling and after there would always be a meal, with much drinking and laughter. During the evenings, they played cards and often discussed national affairs and events and as a child who listened to those conversations around my father's table, I gained a lot of good knowledge. That's how I became educated in the affairs of the world.

The greatest sadness of my young life was when my brother John died in 1740. He was only 23 and I missed him terribly, especially after my sister Mary married Robert Bird and moved away to start a family with him. They had two boys Henry in 1755 and Robert in 1760.

That's how I came to be left alone with my parents. I never married and was happy to remain at Valence in our family's home. I was always grateful to my father for not arranging a marriage, as it probably would have been to an older gentleman, which I would not have liked. That happened to many girls at the time, but my father wanted me to marry only for love and not just for a name or a fortune.

My Father, unlike most, really enjoyed it when he saw I was interested and wanted to engage in conversations about politics and national affairs with his visitors, as he knew I always found those discussions very stimulating.

My nephew Henry, who was such an intelligent young man, was always well prepared and ready for a decent and interesting conversation and as he matured, acquired a very good head for business. He became especially interested in the United States of North America and on becoming a banking agent and trader of securities on the London Market, he quickly built up many connections with important and wealthy men.

In 1775, I remember him discussing the American War of Independence – that was a dreadful war! Going on for years with many people injured and killed on all sides, it continued even after the Declaration of Independence was signed in 1776. It never really ended until 1783.

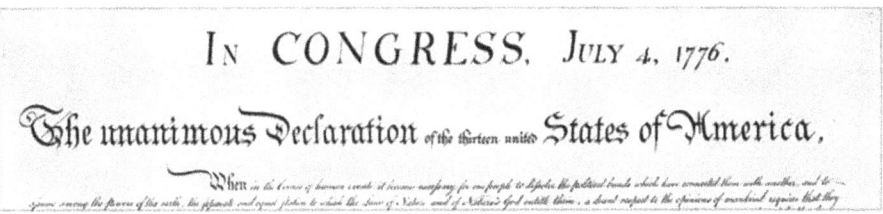

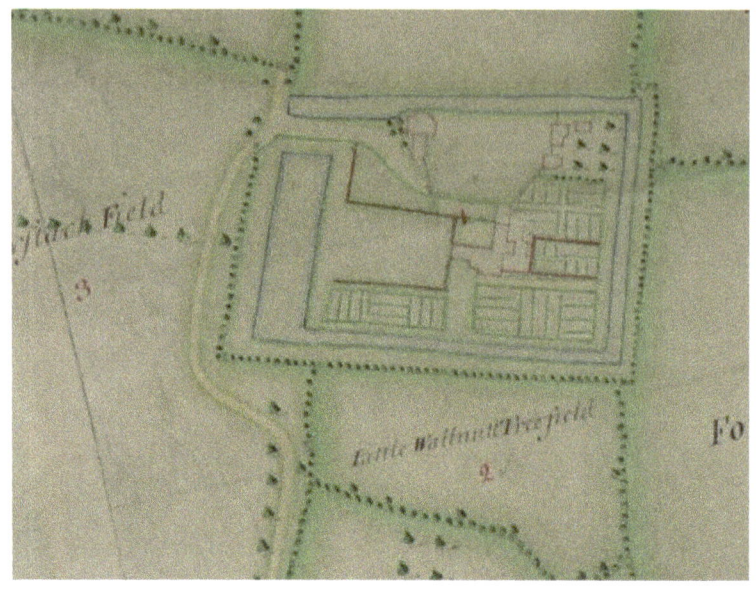

A plan of Valence House in 1771 showing the building, gardens, moat and surrounding fields.

Valence House reconstruction in 1771.

I personally remember the year 1776 with the saddest of memories - it was the year my father died and we buried him in the churchyard of St Peter & St Paul Church in Dagenham Village.

St Peter and St Pauls Church and graveyard.

In his will, I was left our much-loved Valence House, although after he was gone, it was never the same. Of course, I had our very good servants to look after me and keep me company, but I was so very lonely. However, I never imagined that within two years, I would be joining my father in the churchyard of St Peter and St Paul's.

So, I died in January 1778 but could never leave Valence House, I just loved it too much! You might think it strange, but I decided to stay and ever since, I have kept watch over the house…

Of course, a whole new chapter began when my nephew Henry inherited Valence House but as he was like a child of my own, I thought he might need support, so firstly I stayed to watch over him.

Henry was married to Elizabeth Manning, who he liked to call Betsy. She came from a very good family over at Totteridge, but the poor lady was unfortunately often very poorly as she suffered from many ailments. They did not have children, which was sad as I think they would have liked a family.

Marriage certificate of Henry Merttins Bird & Elizabeth Manning.

As Henry and Elizabeth moved into Valence House, I happily saw them settle. Henry, always a good communicator spent much of his time writing letters. Elizabeth also had that talent and I noticed how often they both wrote to Elizabeth's sister Sarah whose husband was Benjamin Vaughan. He was quite an important man and seemed involved on important state business, but all their letters were full of news and gossip. So being an inquisitive person, I read them all and they were really fascinating!

I also watched Henry write his book called *"A View of the Relative Situation of Great Britain and United States of America: by a merchant."* It was a serious book which left me really impressed with his knowledge of American politics and trade.

By reading what he had written, I came to learn how America had secured a treaty with France even though Napoleon was at war with Europe. The terms of the treaty were that no duty was to be paid between France and America on commodities such as tobacco, whale oil, horses, wood, tar, pitch, turpentine, rice, maize or Indian corn, salted fish and bread. On other commodities such as leather, iron, steel, tin, pewter, copper, brass, cotton, wool, hemp, flax, silk etc, the duty was to be priced per ton, but with a reduced price for France and America.

Henry concluded his book on 8th May 1794 by saying "If we must run a race with France for her favour, it is well worth the contest." Later he wrote several other books including *'Proposals of paying off the whole of the present national debt, and for reducing taxes immediately'*.

He was passionate about his business with America, and the subject was frequently discussed over dinner when friends came to stay. He formed a company in London called 'Bird, Savage and Bird' which acted as financiers. I thought it a highly risky business, but there were three partners, himself, Benjamin Savage and his brother Robert Bird and they confidently funded a lot of companies transporting commodities to the U.S.

With many business acquaintances and friends in important positions, it was impressive to see so many letters between him and important men like Rufus King, the American Ambassador in London and Alexander Hamilton, Secretary of the U.S Territory. There were many others too who I know now are considered historically important, but then Henry just counted them among his American friends and connections.

Henry and his partners travelled to the U.S and corresponded via letters to associates and family. So, it is through those family letters that I can tell you much of what happened then, as it came as part of the news of the daily lives of my beloved family.

During 1795, Henry wrote to Sarah Vaughan telling her that her sister Elizabeth's health had come to a low point. *"She had numbness in her hand and tongue from excess of blood. Distension of the excess of the head and difficulty of restoring them to their proper home by them being enclosed in bones which prevents a favourable pressure of the atmosphere and still liable on the least agitation or motion of pleasure or pain or argumentation which may quicken the pulse though only once in a minute to be filled with blood. To counteract the danger, it is necessary to keep her in a most quiet state of dullness and keep her on one floor"*.

Thankfully, Henry was able to engage the help of Mr William MacKinen Frasier, an eminent physician who later became a physician extraordinary to the Prince of Wales. They travelled to Bath especially to see him and he hinted at the probable necessity of cutting off all of Elizabeth's hair so that her head could be braced by the application of cold water. But Elizabeth would have none of that, so the subject had to be instantly dropped as they feared for the consequences of a sudden suffusion of blood over the face. Poor Elizabeth, it was so traumatic, I certainly understand why she said no to that treatment!

Eventually Elizabeth was well enough to travel with Henry to Southend-on-Sea with the hope that fresh air and bathing might improve the health of them both. They stayed at The Terrace on the clifftop at a time before the grand hotels began being built at Southend, as then people with ailments were only starting to discover the medical benefits of visiting this coastal town. Many tired bodies and minds were helped by the 'bracing' sea-air and the 'ozone' said to contain a high amount of oxygen - so vital for a strong constitution.

*The Terrace
Southend on Sea*

*The Terrace and
the Royal Hotel
Southend on Sea*

'The Terrace' was built only one year before Henry & Elizabeth's visit, but when royalty and the aristocracy started to come to Southend it was soon fashionably popular with quality society. In 1802 the hotel was renamed 'The Royal Hotel', following visits made by Princess Caroline, the wife of the Prince Regent.

Henry was so pleased with the view from The Terrace that he said in one of his letters *'it is 60 or 70 feet high up on a cliff and close to the water'* and from there, he reported as seeing the whole navigation of the Thames passing his view at a distance of 3 to 4 miles across the estuary.

All the letters of Henry or Betsy's that I read were interesting, but perhaps the most intriguing were those with news of their brother-in-law Benjamin Vaughan. As a politician sitting in Parliament for the borough of Calne in Wiltshire, he was particularly vocal in stating his views regarding the slave trade and the problems of the plantation owners. I couldn't always agree with his views on slavery, so I was pleased when in February 1794 he came out in favour of the abolition of the slave trade.

But soon after that time, life for Benjamin and his wife Sarah became exceedingly stressful as he was arrested for treason regarding a 'supposed' invasion of England by the French.

It is true that Benjamin was a friend of the French revolutionary politician Robespierre and corresponded with him regularly. However, what caused the trouble for Benjamin was a private letter written to a relative stranger, which became public and resulted in him being accused of spying for the French. Eventually it was found he had only advised that any invasion of England would be impracticable. However, when he was released, he fled to France where he relied upon the protection of Robespierre but very quickly the French state turned suspicious, and then he was accused of spying for William Pitt (the younger) and England!

Taking flight again, Benjamin travelled to Geneva in Switzerland as he realised his former mentor & patron Lord Shelburne could not support him if he returned to London as he no longer had any power, having been ousted out of parliament.

It was then that I heard the news that Sarah and Benjamin Vaughan had a plan to move to America with their children. His family had property and family in Maine as he was not only a British citizen but also an American.

Benjamin Vaughan's American mother Sarah Vaughan, nee Hallowell, and son Richard by Robert Edge Pine (Government Art Collection UK)

You can imagine how sorry I was to see Henry and Elizabeth so upset by that news. Of course, they wished the family well but knew how much they were going to miss them, especially the children. The eldest daughter Harriet was a dear little girl who they loved so very much, for she had bravely suffered illness all her young life.

For a long time, Benjamin was delayed in Switzerland. I understand it was mostly due to his lack of having any passport documents to prove who he was. But not wanting to delay, he managed to let the family know that Sarah with the children must go ahead of him to America.

So naturally, it was Henry who was able to assist with their emigration. That's when the correspondence really got busy! He quickly contacted his many friends in America, while at the same time, he was advising Sarah of the people she must be acquainted with in her new country so they could be entertained and accommodated along their journey.

Watching him prepare his list of who would help and how to seek those introductions was really fascinating. It was then that I realised what an important and influential gentleman trader Henry had become. He numbered among his good friends Rufus King, the lawyer & Senator to Congress; and in Charleston, Philadelphia & New York he was able to ensure that Sarah would have access to the grand drawing rooms of the society hostesses Mrs Pinckney and Mrs Bramford with their coterie of friends and relations.

He also recommended Sarah to Frans Childs, a gentleman connected to Bird, Savage, Bird, as well as Nicholas Cruger, a merchant in New York.

Henry was well known to Alexander Hamilton, the financier and Secretary of the U.S Treasury, and George Washington the first U.S President – remarkable and import men in American history.

In September 1795, Sarah with her children, their tutor and the servants set sail for America. Within days, there was a great storm which caused terrible damage across England and I watched Henry and Elizabeth worry anxiously for the safety of their loved ones out on the Atlantic Ocean. And what happiness and relief they had when joyfully a letter arrived in October to say their family was safely at New York.

They were not long in New York, as news came that in the same month they travelled to Boston. In April 1796 Henry's brother Robert sailed to Philadelphia for business and then travelled northwards to

Boston to join the Vaughan family for a while. It was wonderful to hear all their news coming back.

Benjamin finally managed to find a way to cross to America and was reunited with his family in September that same year. Imagine how joyfully that news was received at Valence House!

The Vaughan family's plan was to become farmers at Hallowell, Kennebeck, Maine and I learnt how that became a reality in the letter of October 1798. I hardly needed to read the letter as Henry and Elizabeth were so excited about the news! I watched and heard them packing gifts that were to be passed on via visiting ships - they especially loved to send seeds for flowers that Sarah could grow and see something familiar from England.

Also, they delighted in hearing of the many different seeds and crops in America and were particularly taken with the ones they called cranberries. This new fruit for English people was soon tasted at Valence House as Henry arranged for a barrel of those berries to be sent over. They were so much enjoyed and talked about at Valence House that I imagined I could taste them!

Trading was Henry's passion and one of his partners, Benjamin Savage, another brother-in-law, started a company in America as Manning & Vaughan, Merchants of London. Through him Sarah's sister was able to arrange the transportation of 6 young pigs, 12 ducks and 12 chickens to add to the livestock at their new home at Hallowell.

Whilst I was watching and hearing of all these events, I noticed that Elizabeth was not looking well. It seems the stress around her family leaving and their difficult journey had taken a toll on her health despite the fact she was still under the care of Dr Fraser. Elizabeth and Henry put their hopes for improved health in a visit to the beautiful spa town Bath. They planned to take 'the waters' and both hoped this treatment would improve Elizabeth's health. It seems that then, when you had stress, this was the very latest way to convalesce and relax.

Henry and Elizabeth were a couple who generally enjoyed living well and I heard they kept a town house in a very fashionable area of London. It was in Guilford Street at Bloomsbury and allowed Henry easy access to his business in the City; but Elizabeth much like me really preferred to be at Valence House with a fresh air lifestyle.

The staircase photographed in 1930 remains in Valence House Today

However, they both enjoyed decorating their houses with the latest fashions and during the years since, I have often paused on the beautiful staircase at Valence House and as I stroke the lovely wood, I remember it was Henry who had it installed.

He had many friends who stayed at Valence, but when John Fiott, a guest from Jersey spent all one evening talking about his business, I was alarmed to hear that it was going bankrupt. When he spoke of his partner Mr De Gruchey from the U.S. being ruined in the "Alley", I worked out that was the name given to the stock market. I kept listening and was worried to hear that Henry had invested a lot of money in the U.S with various companies and individuals.

But for a time, I put that out of my mind and remember enjoying seeing Elizabeth writing to Sarah in December 1796. She was very amused by Sarah's story of how cows on the farm at Hallowell had eaten all her flowers. Elizabeth was not deterred for next time she sent hyacinths - as cows will not eat them!

She was also sending books for the children and was always happy when helping with the children of the family. When she was absent from Valence House for a while, I was surprised to hear she was at Guilford Street taking care of her nephew, little Robert Bird. He had the measles and as his mother had just had another baby he could not be near them as measles is too dangerous for a new-born baby. But with the help of his Aunt Elizabeth, Robert was soon better and back home with his family.

I was pleased to see Elizabeth back in Valence House as she was a good housewife. She was always busy helping around the house making bread or churning butter as well as knitting and spinning as when a young girl she was taught all those skills.

At that time there was always visitors to keep the house alive. Popular guests were the Chitty family with their children and like Elizabeth, I loved watching them play their games in the garden.

Of course, it was not all fun and laughter in the house. Sometimes sad news arrived, and I always sensed when Elizabeth and Henry were upset about things. It was like that when Aunt Lucy Wilberforce died as they were very fond of her and were extremely sad.

Henry spent a lot of his time in London and being a very fashionable man, he decorated his town house in the latest style. Elizabeth would have preferred that he spent more time at Valence House, living a more country life with his farm and socialising pleasantly with their country neighbours. I did notice that when he wrote to Benjamin, he congratulated him on how well he was doing with his farm at Hallowell, but usually their letters were more about scientific philosophy in Europe, the French reformation and religion, and the doctrines of liberty, equality and peace in the world.

Henry was extremely elated by the news of the glorious victory at the mouth of the River Nile when the French flagship called L'Orient was attacked and Bonaparte's expedition fled like a wild goose flight. There was much talk of Admiral Nelson and Captain Darby who as Commander of HMS Bellerophon shared the victory, which I heard, was celebrated throughout all Britain.

About that time, Henry bought Elizabeth a pianoforte. It was such a charming instrument, and she took to music so well that I enjoyed listening to her play. In the evening when Elizabeth & Henry were alone, it was my amusement to watch them playing the game of Whist – can you imagine how funny it was to see all the cards each was holding? They had a lot of pleasure from that game and the cards were often brought out when they had guests.

At one time I heard a lot of talk about Elizabeth's brother having his children inoculated against smallpox. I was worried, but when I heard those little ones were being inoculated by Dr Edward Jenner, I was so pleased as a lot had been written about him. He was such a clever man who found this special way to make what they call 'a vaccine' – the very first in the world. So many people have died of smallpox in recent years - I heard the number was over 400,000 every year. What a wonderful thing Dr Jenner has done!

Edward Jenner FRS. FRCPE (1749-1823) by John Raphael Smith

Elizabeth loved spending time in her garden and although she tended all her flowers, she was especially proud of her roses. Also, there was always an abundance of fruit in the kitchen garden at Valence - the gooseberries and Morello cherries were especially delicious.

Of course, Elizabeth never forgot to save seeds from the gooseberries to send to Sarah.

But like all gardeners, there were disappointments, and I watched her dismay and frustration every time she lost some of her chickens from the hen house when they were carried off by rats of which she could do nothing about.

The year 1799 was one of the saddest I have witnessed during my watch over my family. That year Sarah's sweet elder daughter Harriet died and all shed tears for that dear child.

Robert Bird immediately went out to the U.S. and his wife Lucy with their children followed - I hope they were the comfort they wanted to be to Sarah and her family. Robert's two eldest sons were left in the London house to continue their education and await the return of their mother and their younger brothers and sisters.

I felt such pity for Elizabeth. She loved Harriet so much and longed to go with Lucy and the children to offer comfort to her sister. But an attack of lumbago came on exactly at that time and all she could do was send seeds for Sarah and books and toys for the children. During this time, I was careful to watch over Elizabeth as her sadness brought her spirit so low that she just spent hours sitting by the fire.

Across the Atlantic, Sarah eventually found a way through her grief by writing and making books to set up a lending library for the education of children. This was a serious matter for Sarah & Benjamin Vaughan for together they provoked their young family to learn through asking questions. This 'Enlightened' method aimed to build curiosity into intelligent young minds and by their inclusion in family discussions from an early age, they hoped a child would learn to understand their roles and responsibilities in society.

Taking her lending library in a cart, Sarah Vaughan travelled around her community distributing not only books but also clothes and food. As her books became well used, Sarah personally sewed and bound them back together and her commitment to education in her community left a legacy well beyond her lifetime.

With time as a healer, the company of Robert Bird, his wife and their seven healthy children, brought a renewed pleasure to Henry and Elizabeth. Their family visits to Valence House were a time when the house rang with merriment.

Yet, sadly, in 1800 and 1801, especially during the winter months, Elizabeth was a very serious invalid. I gathered she had a defective digestion which reduced her in flesh, strength and spirits, and coupled with rheumatoid pain she could find no energy for interest in her flowers or vegetable garden.

Henry writing to Sarah seemed concerned to give her advice about lending money to people. Through his work as an agent banker and security trader he well understood the risks involved when lending money and told her how a niece's husband had become bankrupt. I also read that he told her how he had secured for the niece a separate maintenance of £300 per year from her grandfather's investment of a house in the West Indies. This would have keep them comfortable in retirement in the country, but sadly it came too late, for her child had already been taken from her to be brought up by her husband's mother and sister.

The beginning of 1803 brought Henry the news that his mother had been unwell and was writing her will to provide for her family. But personal fortune had already turned against her sons as Henry had become ill, and his brother Robert Bird was penniless.

Bird, Savage and Bird had lent vast amounts of money to companies in America and debts were not being paid especially in Massachusetts. Robert had just enough money for bread and meat to feed his family – and his brother and partner Henry was not in any better position to lend him any money.

I understood more about their problems when I saw the brief letter from Henry to Benjamin Vaughan in the U.S.A. It spoke of a definitive treaty and numerous large sums of money in amounts that sounded frighteningly large and absurd. Who could imagine loans of 25 million and 97 million with 4 million taxes and funds that needed to be raised in a week amounting to 68 to 78 million?

I understood that the companies and people to whom money had been lent had not paid their debts, so consequently Bird, Savage and Bird were themselves in debt. Alarmingly, Henry's business would not allow him to go to America, so he could only wait for his certificate of bankruptcy while his creditors allowed him only £600 per year to act as an agent for their own affairs.

Every event during those days seemed be a confusion. I even heard there was much talk about a possible invasion of Hanover by the French army. This was very alarming as our King George III was also the Elector of Hanover so it was generally assumed that any such invasion would also be a personal attack on Britain.

Our army was put on alert and as Henry was in the Bloomsbury Corps, he became much engaged in drilling his men ready to defend against the French. The corps, sometimes called the Bloomsbury Rifles, was from 1803 & 1814 made up of volunteers, but were still considered part of the British Army.

Then there was another piece of news which really frightened us all - Henry's nephew, Henry Bird who was in the Navy became shipwrecked a month after sailing from England but thanks to God, that poor young fellow's life was preserved along with the rest of the crew. He bravely chose to go to sea again and I heard he had gone on board Captain Hardyman's ship, the Unicorn a good strong frigate built in 1794 at Chatham Dockyard. Strangely, I heard they did not know where he was sailing to - but we all kept praying he was safe. He was only 13 years old then, what an excellent, brave young boy! His new ship, seems to have been a very reliable vessel, for even as late as 1903 it was sailing the North Sea and cruising around the Caribbean.

All these troubles took a toll on Henry & Elizabeth, and by June 1804 both were unwell. With hopes of improving her health, Elizabeth went to Brighton to bathe while Henry chose the benefits of again drinking the waters at Bath, to try to overcome a bilious complaint. The stress of bankruptcy, and the deaths of both his mother and uncle, had obviously affected their health.

However, despite poor health, Henry was still thinking and worrying about Sarah and Benjamin in America. When he heard of Yellow Fever on Long Island, close to New York and the possibly it could come to Maine, he was greatly concerned. As far as I understand that horrible sickness was carried by ships from the Caribbean and passed on by the mosquitoes.

Eventually, whilst I roamed about the house in my usual way, I caught the whisper of the rumour that Henry had made a gentleman's agreement regarding Valence House with John Hopkins Dare.

I heard that John Hopkins Dare had purchased the house in 1802 with the proviso that Henry would be able to buy it back when he had raised the funds. As you can imagine, I was very worried but still hopeful because I knew how hard Henry was working to collect debts for the creditors.

Sadly, poor Henry, was not successful and finally had to admit he was unable to raise the funds. So, our beloved Valence House was put up for auction in 1804.

NOtice is hereby given, that the Partnerſhip between us Henry Merttins Bird and Benjamin Savage, under the Firm of Bird and Savage, was this Day diſſolved by mutual Conſent; and all Debts due to or owing by the ſaid Partnerſhip will be received and paid by the ſaid Henry Merttins Bird, who is charged with the Liquidation of the Concerns of the ſaid Partnerſhip. Witneſs our Hands this 31ſt Day of March 1808,   *H. M. Bird.*
Ben. Savage.

The notice of sale gave a good description of our lovely home but how could it describe the love contained within the walls?

Valence House

Attic storey
five servant's apartments.

First storey
five good bed chambers, two dressing rooms neatly fitted & good convenient closets.

Ground floor
dining parlour, breakfast parlour, entrance hall & two staircases.

The Offices
good kitchen, scullery fitted with ovens, butler pantry, storeroom, laundry, wash house, cool dairy, cellars.
Poultry yard with a range of hen houses, fore court, spacious yard with coach and chaise house, harness house, granary, pigeon house, Stable and loft,
Farmyard with cow house and cattle shed and piggery.
Lawn & pleasure ground neatly laid out in gravel walks with shrubbery borders, green house, good gardens cropped & planted with walled & standard fruit trees bearing fruit & orchard, melon ground, Tool house, fishponds, meadow, pasture and arable land with timber.

The Lot was sold for £15,000!

Watching Henry and Elizabeth pack and leave our beloved house I cried along with them.

Fortunately, they were eventually able to settle and live quietly at Barton-on-the-Heath, Stratford upon Avon, Warwickshire.

Elizabeth died in 1817, and Henry the following year when a memorial plaque was put up in the parish church at Barton-on-the Heath.

Yet, Valence House and Dagenham stayed in his heart as at his request he was buried with his family at the parish church of St Peter and St Paul in the village.

…so now I am left to draw down the curtain on our family's story but I hope I have opened your eyes to let you 'see' our lives a little clearer?

As for myself, well I am staying around - so don't be surprised if you sense a friend enfolding you as you wander through Valence House and gardens. Remember *'the loving spirit lingers long and would not pass away'.*

Bird Memorial Window
St. Lawrence Church
Barton-on-the-Heath

Acknowledgments

This work of fiction is inspired by the correspondence generated between the Merttin Bird family at Valence House and their relatives, the Vaughan family at Hallowell, Maine, United States of America, in the period 1795 to 1804.

(Massachusetts Historical Society – Vaughan Family papers – Call Number MS. N-83) – copies available at Valence House Archives and Local Studies, Dagenham.

Other sources

The Valence House Estate in the 18th Century, *'The Merttins: a country estate for prosperous city merchants'*.

Vaughan Homestead Today, Sarah's Lending library
https://exhibits.amphilsoc.org/sarah-manning-vaughan/exhibits/show/sarah-manning-vaughan/sarah-vaughan-lending-library

Copies of Parish records St Peter & St Paul Dagenham Church held at Valence House Archives and Local Studies

National Institutes of Health, National Library of Medicines
https://www.ncbi.nlm.nih.gov

Royal College of Physicians written by William Munk
https://history.rcplondon.ac.uk/inspiring-physicians/william-mackinen-fraser

'A View of a Relative Situation of Great Britain and the United States of North America: by a merchant' 1794 Henry Merttins Bird.

https://www.historyofparliamentonline.org/volume/1790-1820/member/vaughan-benjamin-1751-1820

London Gazette – 29th March 1808 Page 461

https://www.southendtimeline.co.uk/4/southend-timeline-health-resort-history-of-southend-on-sea.html

Photos of The Terrace Southend on Sea, Mark Percy, Billericay archives.

https://www.southendtimeline.co.uk/southend-timeline-a-seaside-town-brief-history-history-of-southend-on-sea.html

https://www.britainexpress.com/counties/warwickshire/churches/barton-on-the-heath.htm

Wikipedia.com

Title inspired by *'Self-Interrogation'* by Emily Bronte (1846).

'Alas! the countless links are strong
That bind us to our clay;
The loving spirit lingers long,
And would not pass away!'

Other images not listed above are copyright of Valence House Archives and Local Studies.

The Archives & Local Studies Centre at Valence House, has for many years been the hub of historical research for the London Borough of Barking & Dagenham and among the vast archives are many collections of letters relating to resident families dating back 400 years.

Whilst transcribing letters between Henry Merttins Bird and the Vaughan family, as researchers we began to imagine how events took place at Valence House during their time. We were then inspired to create a scenario which evolved into this publication. All the events mentioned concerning the two families who were living in England and America, are factual and reflect the correspondence. The emotions involved and the possibility of a loving family member's spirit remaining to safeguard her family and home, are entirely fictional.

This new adventure in producing a work of fiction based on fact we hope will find favour as we have ideas to explore the stories of other spirits that may remain within the walls of Valence House.

Deirdre Marculescu, Rosalind Alexander & Derek Alexander

www.ingramcontent.com/pod-product-compliance
Lightning Source LLC
Chambersburg PA
CBHW061226070526
44584CB00029B/4010